Words
Every Woman
Should Remember

We wish to thank Susan Polis Schutz for permission to reprint the following poems that appear in this publication: "The love of a family...," "Find happiness in nature...," "Be a woman who...," "You are a remarkable woman...," "Successful people have these twelve...," "Some people will be your friend...," "Give yourself the freedom...," "If you ever find yourself...," and "You have to find a way...." Copyright © 1982, 1983, 1984, 1986, 1988, 2004 by Stephen Schutz and Susan Polis Schutz. And for "Many people go...." Copyright © 1980 by Continental Publications. All rights reserved.

Library of Congress Control Number: 2012939804
ISBN: 978-1-59842-684-7

▶️ and Blue Mountain Press are registered in U.S. Patent and Trademark Office.
Certain trademarks are used under license.

Acknowledgments appear on page 92.

Printed in China.
Fourth Printing: 2014

♻ This book is printed on recycled paper.

This book is printed on paper that has been specially produced to be acid free (neutral pH) and contains no groundwood or unbleached pulp. It conforms with the requirements of the American National Standards Institute, Inc., so as to ensure that this book will last and be enjoyed by future generations.

Blue Mountain Arts, Inc.
P.O. Box 4549, Boulder, Colorado 80306

Words Every Woman Should Remember

Messages of Support, Encouragement,
and Gratitude for All You Are
and All You Do

Edited by
Patricia Wayant

Blue Mountain Press™
Boulder, Colorado

Words
Every Woman
Should Remember...

*T*he greatest gift you've been given is you.
Celebrate yourself... with hope, with joy,
with appreciation. Dare to dream. Open your
heart and let yourself go as far as your mind
will take you. Drop any regrets and negative
thoughts that hold you down. Count your
blessings; love your life; treasure your family
and friends and all that you're thankful for.
Above all, soak in the gift of each moment
and enjoy it with all your heart.

— Donna Fargo

- ⑤ *You are somebody's hero.*

- ⑤ *Be true to yourself... trust your instincts.*

- ⑤ *You work hard and deserve more recognition than you get.*

- ⑤ *The only one responsible for your life is you.*

- ⑤ *You have changed the world in immeasurable ways.*

- ⑤ *You are beautiful, admirable, and strong.*

Look in the mirror and
see what others see —
a talented, uplifting,
and magnificent woman
who can do anything
and everything she wants.

Believe in your heart
that you have the power
to grab hold of your future
and mold it into the things
you have always dreamed of.

Trust in your soul
that you are capable of doing
all that needs to be done.

Know that you are
incredible in every way
and see yourself
as others see you...
as an intelligent
and spectacular woman.

— Lamisha Serf

There are women who make things better... simply by showing up. There are women who make things happen. There are women who make their way. There are women who make a difference. There are women who make us smile. There are women who do not make excuses and women who cannot be replaced. There are women of wit and wisdom who — through strength and courage — make it through. There are women who change the world every day... women like you.

— Ashley Rice

◎ *Every big change starts with a small step.*

◎ *If you don't like how things are going, do something about it!*

◎ *Helping others is one of the greatest acts you can do.*

◎ *Every day has the potential to be amazing.*

◎ *The world relies on women like you.*

You're a one-of-a-kind treasure, uniquely here in this space and time. You are here to shine in your own wonderful way, sharing your smile in the best way you can, and remembering all the while that a little light somewhere makes a brighter light everywhere. You can — and you do — make a wonderful contribution to this world.

You have qualities within you that many people would love to have, and those who really and truly know you... are so glad that they do. You have a big heart and a good and sensitive soul. You are gifted with thoughts and ways of seeing things that only special people know.

You know that life doesn't always play by the rules but that in the long run, everything will work out.

You understand that you and your actions are capable of turning anything around — and that joys once lost can always be found. There is a resolve and an inner reserve of strength in you that few ever get to see. You have so many treasures within — those you're only beginning to discover, and all the ones you're already aware of.

Never forget what a treasure you are. That special person in the mirror may not always get to hear all the compliments you so sweetly deserve, but you are so worthy of such an abundance... of friendship, joy, and love.

— Douglas Pagels

*D*ay in and day out, you make the world a better place to be. And the people who are lucky enough to be in your life are the ones who get to see that you're a very wonderful person with a truly gifted touch. You go a million miles out of your way, and you always do so much to make sure that other lives are easier and filled with happiness. Your caring could never be taken for granted because the people you're close to are blessed with someone who works at a job well done to bring smiles to the day.

— Jenn Davids

◎ *Your presence adds something special and invaluable to the world. You bring joy to those who love you and a smile to everyone you meet.*
(Star Nakamoto)

◎ *Over a lifetime, it's the moments you take to help a friend in need, push a child on a swing, or encourage someone else's dream that will be remembered.*

◎ *All the small things you do every day add up to something pretty significant.*

◎ *You inspire others with your kindness and compassion.*

◎ *The greatest gifts you can give are the ones that come from your heart.*

🌀 *Recognize and appreciate your own talents.*

🌀 *It matters what you think. Speak up. Voice your opinions. Share your ideas.*

🌀 *Choose your goals purposefully.*

🌀 *Be proud of all you've achieved.*

🌀 *As soon as you trust yourself, you will know how to live. (Johann Wolfgang von Goethe)*

There is no one in the past, present, or future who will ever offer the world what you do. No one will think, act, or smile exactly like you. No one will be able to come up with your unique points of view.

Don't hold back who you really are. When you are true to yourself, you glow. When you are passionate about your dreams, you shine. When you live fully, people are drawn to you. And then you can't help but make friends with good people: the ones who love you for just being you.

— April Aragam

*S*trong women are those who know the road ahead will be strewn with obstacles, but they still choose to walk it because it's the right one for them.

Strong women are those who make mistakes, who admit to them, learn from those failures, and then use that knowledge.

Strong women are easily hurt, but they still extend their hearts and hands, knowing the risk and accepting the pain when it comes.

Strong women are sometimes beat down by life, but they still stand back up and step forward again.

Strong women are afraid. They face fear and move ahead to the future, as uncertain as it can be.

Strong women are not those who succeed the first time. They're the ones who fail time and again, but still keep trying until they succeed.

Strong women face the daily trials of life, sometimes with a tear, but always with their heads held high as the new day dawns.

— Brenda Hager

- *If you are doing the best you can, then that's all you can do.*

- *Don't let your fears prevent you from pursuing your dreams.*

- *You must do the thing you think you cannot do.* (Eleanor Roosevelt)

- *Worry never solves anything.*

- *Go where your heart tells you to go.*

There is a vitality, a life-force, an energy, a quickening that is translated through you into action. And because there is only one of you in all time, this expression is unique. And if you block it, it will never exist through any other medium and be lost. The world will not have it. It is not your business to determine how good it is, nor how valuable, nor how it compares with other expressions. It is your business to keep it yours clearly and directly, to keep the channel open.

— Martha Graham

Be a woman who
knows what she wants to do
and does it
A woman who
is not afraid to
speak out for what she believes
A woman who
is kind and good and giving
A woman who
sets high goals for herself
and achieves them
A woman who
is beautiful on the outside
and the inside
A woman who
understands herself and
is in complete charge of her life
A woman who
is intelligent and sensitive
strong and able
A woman who
gives so much to her friends
to her family
to everyone

— Susan Polis Schutz

🌀 Don't be afraid to show the world your true, authentic self.

🌀 By being yourself, you help others to be themselves.

🌀 One act of kindness can lead to another and then another, and you can be the person to start it off.

🌀 You deserve complete and total respect.

🌀 It's not what you do but who you are that counts.

*It's easy to get caught up
in everyday life —
racing the clock, meeting deadlines,
shuffling the workload,
and becoming so focused
on what you "do" that
you forget to simply "be."*

*Remember to stop and take time for you.
The world will not fall apart
or leave you behind if you allow yourself
a few moments of quiet.*

*There is no need for stress and struggle.
Everything that is meant to be will be —
with or without your help.*

*So relax, find your balance,
live fully in each moment,
and remember... breathe.*

— Lisa Butler

⊚ *To put the world in order, we must first put the nation in order; to put the nation in order, we must first put the family in order; to put the family in order, we must first cultivate our personal life; and to cultivate our personal life, we must first set our hearts right. (Confucius)*

⊚ *Take a little time every day just for yourself — even if it's only fifteen minutes.*

⊚ *Allow plenty of room for what matters most in your life — love, friendship, family, and laughter.*

⊚ *Have fun every chance you get.*

⟳ Every woman needs a place she can call her own — whether it's a whole room, a spot in the garden, or a special chair — where she can relax and be herself.

⟳ The peace you are looking for is inside yourself.

⟳ Don't commit yourself to a project just because it's what others want you to do. Be sure it's something you want too.

⟳ You're not being selfish when you do something nice for yourself.

Don't just have minutes in the day, have moments in time. Balance out any bad with the good you can provide. Know that you are capable of amazing results. Surprise yourself by discovering new strength inside.

Do things no one else would even dream of. There is no greater gift than the kind of inner beauty you possess. Do the things you do... with love.

Walk along the pathways that enrich your happiness. Taking care of the "little things" is a big necessity. Don't be afraid of testing your courage. Life is short, but it's long enough to have excitement and serenity.

Don't let the important things go unsaid. Do the things that brighten your life and help you on your way.

— *Collin McCarty*

Set a goal each day
to walk a less-traveled road,
praise an unsung hero,
reach an impossible dream.
Set a goal to make time just for you
to read, reflect, and renew;
to find healing in silence
and comfort through prayer;
to exercise your mind and body
so that your health will stay strong,
your creativity high,
and your spirit alive.

Set a goal to be thankful
for the smallest pleasures
and open to the greatest miracles,
to step outside yourself
to make someone's day
a little brighter
and the world a little kinder.

Set a goal each day
to share your strength
with those who stumble
and your faith
with those who fear —
to connect with another soul
and listen more closely to your own.
Set a goal to forgive the past,
trust the future,
live in the moment,
and find each moment worthwhile —
and to remember that strength
comes from striving,
courage from doing,
and peace from knowing
that you can never go wrong
when you go with your heart.

— Paula Finn

Stretching herself too thin, a woman breaks her connections.

Staying too busy, she has no time.

Doing for others, she neglects herself.

Defining herself only through others, she loses her own definition.

The wise woman waters her own garden first.

— Nu Shu Proverb

- *Superwoman is a fictional character; she does not actually exist.*

- *It's okay if the house isn't always clean.*

- *The more you rush around, the more behind you get.*

- *Preserving your sanity is more important than meeting a deadline.*

- *You are limited by the number of things you can do at once.*

- *You can — and will — check off every item on your to-do list in time.*

There will be times in life that test your patience and resolve, but even when things don't seem to be working out for the best, you can still make the best of them.

Focus on your goals, try to learn all you can, and keep an open mind and heart. Be receptive enough to recognize an opportunity you might not have imagined, and be flexible enough to change your direction if you need to. Remember to stay committed to what you want to accomplish, and don't be discouraged.

Don't let one test or one result define you. Don't let one disappointment make you think you've lost the war when it was only a single battle. When you make mistakes, learn from them. Making decisions in the face of conflict helps you to know yourself better. Consciously changing your attitude from frustration to fascination will empower you. Embrace every challenge and don't worry.

Be patient, keep on doing your best, and one day, probably when you're least expecting it, the best will come to you.

— Donna Fargo

⑥ *Nobody's life is without challenges and hardships, bad days and even worse days, but everybody gets a shot at new days and second chances.*

⑥ *You're going to make some mistakes — don't dwell on them.*

⑥ *There are some things you cannot change — accept that and move on.*

⑥ *Don't let setbacks and disappointments discourage you — you have untapped reserves of inner strength.*

⑥ *Let any regrets you may have be a springboard for your future.*

*S*ometimes the hardest times
in our lives are what push us
further, inspire us to be bolder,
teach us about real hope, dreams,
and how to believe... They help us to
become the greatest version of that
person we always hoped we'd be.

No matter what circumstance,
state, or place you may find yourself
in some days, just keep being you: a
bold, bright star.

— Ashley Rice

Embrace change, and you'll keep on growing forever. Keep making new friends, and your circle will constantly expand. Nurture the talents of others, and you'll always get results.

Be a promise keeper, and you'll keep people's trust. Be who you are, and you'll always be real. Give credit to those who helped you reach goals, and you'll always have a team.

Keep aiming high, and you'll always have dreams. Keep your eyes open, and you'll see opportunities. Keep your enthusiasm, and you'll always be inspired. Be patient and persistent, and you won't ever feel the need to quit. Seek help when you need it, and you'll never struggle alone.

*Keep your energy, passion, and excitement
for life, and you'll never be bored or discontented.
Stay focused on your goals and not on who others
want you to be or what they want you to achieve.*

*When making decisions, listen to your logical
mind, but don't leave behind the wisdom of your
instincts and the messages from your heart. Listen
to all of them, and do what's right for you. Let
your faith be a guiding light and daily comfort,
and you will always feel blessed.*

— *Jacqueline Schiff*

*T*here are two very easy things
   to do in life:
One is to blame someone else
for anything and everything,
the other is to make excuses to yourself.
That's just the way life is.
Either way, you deny yourself
of truly being responsible
for your own life and your own happiness.
Quit making excuses.
Be the person you really want to be,
and know that the fewer excuses you make,
the better you will feel about
all the rewards that come your way.

— Deanna Beisser

- *Whatever you are trying to avoid won't go away until you confront it. (Author Unknown)*

- *Spend less time agonizing over decisions and more time acting on what you think needs to be done.*

- *Be open to views and opinions that are different from your own.*

- *Advice is one of the easiest things to give and the hardest things to receive.*

- *No one can make you feel inferior without your consent. (Eleanor Roosevelt)*

⑤ *Life is an adventure, dare it.* (Mother Teresa)

⑤ *Look into your heart, search your dreams, and be honest about what you really want; then do whatever it takes to get it. Live like you mean it. Believe you can... and you will!* (Barbara Cage)

⑤ *Step out of your comfort zone sometimes — you might discover something new about yourself.*

⑤ *The future depends on what we do in the present.* (Mahatma Gandhi)

*You don't have to have all
the answers or always know
the right thing to say. You can climb
the highest mountain if you want...
or quietly imagine that you might
someday. You can take chances or
take safety nets, make miracles or
make mistakes. You don't have to be
composed at all hours to be strong.
You don't have to be bold or certain
to be brave.*

— *Ashley Rice*

𝒴ou have all the resources you need to see you through anything. You are a courageous person who has faced one challenge after another and always came bouncing back with a smile on your face.

You are so much bigger than you think you are. Whatever it takes, you can do it.

— Lynda Field

⑥ The best protection any woman can have...
is courage. *(Elizabeth Cady Stanton)*

⑥ There is no such thing as failure — only
lessons learned.

⑥ Sometimes it is out of our greatest fears
that come our most beneficial experiences.

⑥ Always have something to hope for.

⑥ Miracles happen when you least expect them.

⑥ *You have to find a way to balance your work, private life, and everything else that is important to you.* (Susan Polis Schutz)

⑥ *Don't get stuck repeating the same mistakes — whether it's your lifestyle, your diet, or your relationships.*

⑥ *Don't ever downplay your abilities or your special charm. Keep living your life the best way you know how — with persistence, patience, and determination.* (Vickie M. Worsham)

⑥ *When your heart is in the right place, you can never go wrong.*

⑥ *Act as if what you do makes a difference. It does.* (William James)

*To be good at any one thing
requires discipline.*

*To be great at any one thing
demands commitment.*

*To reach your goals
and to obtain your dreams...*

You must never stop trying.

— *Deanna Beisser*

*When you get into a tight
place and everything goes
against you until it seems that you
cannot hold on for a minute longer,
never give up then, for that is just the
place and time when the tide will turn.*

— *Harriet Beecher Stowe*

*S*uccessful people have these
twelve qualities in common
They have confidence in themselves
They have a very strong sense of purpose
They never have excuses for not doing something
They always try their hardest for perfection
They never consider the idea of failing
They work extremely hard toward their goals
They know who they are
They understand their weaknesses
as well as their strong points
They can accept and benefit from criticism
They know when to defend what they are doing
They are creative
They are not afraid to be a little different
in finding innovative solutions
that will enable them to achieve their dreams

— Susan Polis Schutz

⑥ *Success is often a personal achievement that goes beyond material wealth and reputation. It can be something as rewarding as making a nourishing meal for your family or growing a flower garden from seed.*

⑥ *To guarantee success, act as if it were impossible to fail. (Dorothea Brande)*

⑥ *Energy and persistence conquer all things. (Benjamin Franklin)*

⑥ *The most important thing in our lives is what we are doing now. (Author Unknown)*

There are times when it can feel
like your dreams are so far away
that you will never reach them,
no matter how much you work
or how hard you try.
In those moments... relax,
go with the flow,
and follow your heart's desires.
The answers will come
and you'll know what to do next.
Just take it one step at a time.

You don't need to struggle
for what you want.
Be joyful and believe that
you are worthy of your dreams —
and they will find you every time,
because you deserve them all.

— Lisa Butler

- Schedule time in your day when you can let your body and mind be at total rest.

- Fear less, hope more; eat less, chew more; whine less, breathe more; talk less, say more; hate less, love more; and all good things are yours. (Swedish Proverb)

- Adopt the pace of nature: her secret is patience. (Ralph Waldo Emerson)

- When you accept what is — without any judgment — you will find serenity.

- There's only one rule you need to remember: laugh at everything and forget everybody else! (Anne Frank)

Refuse negative thoughts;
*   replace them with positive ones.*
Look for the good things in your life
and make a point of appreciating them.
Believe in yourself and know that you
*   have the power.*
You are ultimately the one in charge
*   of your life*
and the only person in the world who
*   can change it.*
No matter how much others are
*   pulling for you*
or how much anyone else cares,
you must do what needs to be done
to make your present and future
everything you want and need it to be.

— Barbara Cage

- *You are in control of your own thoughts.*

- *The happiest people are those who look out on the world with a positive mindset. They focus on what they have, instead of what they don't have, and find joy in life's simplest pleasures.*

- *Fretting over the past will get you nowhere fast.*

- *Within the scope of the universe, it's likely that the very thing causing you the most stress is actually very insignificant.*

- *Embrace what is good in your life, and let go of the rest.*

By turning your disappointments around, you can make them into open doors instead. By closing the doors to the past, you can reinvent yourself with a new vision.

Make new dreams where the old dreams have slipped away, and build hope for a better tomorrow. Changes can occur when you least expect them, and the worst day of your life can also turn out to be the best day of your life.

— *Jeanie Turocy*

*G*ather up your doubts,
  your fears,
and your "what ifs," "I can'ts,"
and second-guesses.
Embrace them.
Thank them for
their thoughtfulness
and concern.
Then blow them
a gentle kiss goodbye,
and go out and show the world
what you've got!
                    — Robin Magon

◎ Notice serendipitous moments and events happening in your life. They may be trying to tell you something.

◎ Accept help from others when it's offered; offer help to others when you can.

◎ Spend more time with the positive people in your life, and less time with the negative ones.

◎ Sometimes it is simply best just to wait and see what happens. *(George Sand)*

There are angels among us.
You may have encountered
one lately.
It may have been someone
who offered an encouraging word,
a helping hand,
or a simple smile.
Angels know how to touch
through human hands
and love through human hearts.
It doesn't take a miracle to recognize
when an angel has been at work.
Just open your eyes
and watch for love in action.
Angels are everywhere.
Seen or unseen, they lift spirits,
encourage the downhearted,
and offer heavenly help
for down-to-earth problems.

If you hear the sound of wings, remember:
angels are watching over you.

— Candy Paull

*E*ach new day is a blank page in the diary of your life. Every day you're given a chance to determine what the words will say and how the story will unfold.

If you work it right, the story of your life will be a wonderful one. The more rewarding you can make each page, the more exquisite the entire book will be.

Remember: goodness will be rewarded. Smiles will pay you back. Have fun. Find strength. Be truthful. Have faith. Don't focus on anything you lack.

Have a diary that describes how you are doing your best, and... the rest will take care of itself.

— Douglas Pagels

🌀 *Give yourself the freedom to try out new things. Don't be so set in your ways that you can't grow. (Susan Polis Schutz)*

🌀 *The difference between ordinary and extraordinary is that little extra. (Author Unknown)*

🌀 *Be open to new ideas, new people, and new adventures.*

🌀 *Every now and then, go ahead and do something wild and outrageous!*

🌀 *Dance like nobody's watching; love like you've never been hurt. Sing like nobody's listening; live like it's heaven on earth. (Author Unknown)*

⊚ *Have something unique in your life that's just for you — whether it's a special interest, a particular hobby, or a favorite tradition.*

⊚ *When the road curves to lead you into new discoveries... let it take you. When the wind pulls under your wings and urges you on to greater heights... let it take you. (Susan A. J. Lyttek)*

⊚ *Remember how it was to be a child. Take your shoes off! Explore! Play a game! Let your imagination transport you to wherever you want to go!*

⊚ *It's okay to color outside the lines.*

⊚ *Be happy now!*

*F*ind happiness in nature
  in the beauty of a mountain
in the serenity of the sea
Find happiness in friendship
in the fun of doing things together
in the sharing and understanding
Find happiness in your family
in the stability of knowing
    that someone cares
in the strength of love and honesty
Find happiness in yourself
in your mind and body
in your values and achievements
Find happiness in
everything
you
do

— Susan Polis Schutz

Try to do these things every day...
Believe in angels.
You're one of them.
Count your blessings —
starting with the one you are.
Hug yourself.
Take joy in the treasure you are.
Be as good to yourself as you
so often are to others.
Let your dreams grow as high
as the sky.
Smile into the sun and let it
smile back at you.
Put your feet up.
Open your heart
to the love all around you.
Celebrate the beautiful person you are,
because inside and out,
there's no one else like you.

Open up the windows of your life
and let joy shine in.
You really are the treasure
at rainbow's end.
Do something fun.
Do the things that give you goose bumps.
Call yourself "amazing"…
because that's what you are.
Picture a perfect day…
then make it your own.
You deserve every sunbeam
this day has to offer.
You bring gifts to each day
and smiles to each heart,
and no one is more special than you.

— Linda E. Knight

*The things that matter in this life
are not fortune and fame.
They are only temporary solutions.
True happiness comes from within
when we appreciate all
we have been blessed with —
knowing that we do not need more.
You are loved, appreciated,
and very special.
You have touched so many lives
and made this world a better place
just by being the one-of-a-kind,
beautiful person that you are.*

— Jason Blume

◎ *Don't try to be something you're not.*

◎ *Real happiness comes from knowing who you are and being the best that you can be.*

◎ *Accept compliments when they are given.*

◎ *Appreciation is a wonderful thing; it makes what is excellent in others belong to us as well. (Voltaire)*

◎ *Fill your heart with the kindness of friends, the caring of everyone you love, and the richness of memories you wouldn't trade for anything. (Douglas Pagels)*

⑥ Take time each day to think about the blessings in your life.

⑥ Find at least one thing every day to be grateful for.

⑥ Every day, be full of awareness of the beauty around you. Be full of gratitude for friends and family, for the goodness you find in others, for your health and all you're capable of. (Barbara Cage)

⑥ Joy is not in things; it is in us. (Richard Wagner)

*G*ratitude unlocks the fullness of life.
Gratitude makes things right. It
turns what we have into enough, and
more. It turns denial into acceptance,
chaos to order, confusion to clarity. It
can turn a meal into a feast, a house
into a home, a stranger into a friend. It
turns problems into gifts, failures into
successes, the unexpected into perfect
timing, and mistakes into important
events. It can turn an existence into a
real life, and disconnected situations into
important and beneficial lessons.
Gratitude makes sense of our past,
brings peace for today, and creates a
vision for tomorrow.

— Melody Beattie

So often, it's the little things in life
that make the biggest difference...
Sometimes a word offered
at the perfect moment
can bring someone comfort.
A hug wrapped in loving arms
sends a caring message to the heart,
and one smile can chase the blues away
and make you smile again too.

A little time shared with someone
who cares about you
can sprinkle sunshine into lonely moments
by letting someone know how much
they mean to you.

Life offers many opportunities
to give away a little of ourselves
    each day —
to share the joy of life
and living in this world together,
to widen that circle of friendship
wherever we go.

If we could all make a point
of remembering those little things,
we could all make a difference every day.

A well-placed word, a tender touch,
a heartfelt hug, a sincere smile...
are ways to spread sunshine
all along life's path.

— Barbara J. Hall

*It's so easy for women to slip into
self-doubt and feeling inadequate.
After all,
we shoulder a lot of responsibilities —
    being supportive of our mates,
    nurturing our children,
    staying in touch with extended family,
    holding down jobs
    while holding down the fort at home.*

*No wonder we sometimes feel
    anxious, exhausted, and insecure.*

*We need to know
    we're not alone.
We need to hear
    that other women share our experiences.
We need reassurance
    that there's someone who understands —
    someone who's been there, done that.*

*As women, we take turns encouraging,
    supporting, and cheering one another on.*

— BJ Gallagher

◎ Always have at least one true friend you can talk with about anything.

◎ We don't make it alone in this world. We're lucky that there are people placed in our path to guide us, protect us, and touch our lives. *(Julia Escobar)*

◎ Learn from the women who came before you.

◎ Remember that a heart is like a garden that needs to be tended to and nourished with what only another heart can give — love and appreciation, devotion and honesty. *(Tracia Gloudemans)*

*S*ome people will be your friend
because of whom you know
Some people will be your friend
because of your position
Some people will be your friend
because of the way you look
Some people will be your friend
because of your possessions
But the only real friends
are the people who will be your friends
because they like you for how you are inside

— Susan Polis Schutz

🌀 *Surround yourself with people who will support and encourage you and who make you feel good.*

🌀 *Be a good listener — sometimes all the person you're listening to really wants is to be heard.*

🌀 *Celebrate your friendships. Make time to get together with a special friend.*

🌀 *Look for the good in others — everybody has his or her own song to sing. Give people a chance to love you, for that is how you learn to love.*
(Melissa Ososki)

Women's Declaration of Interdependence

We hold these truths to be self-evident:

That all women are created equal, but each is blessed with different gifts and talents.

That all women are endowed with certain individual rights, but each must assume shared responsibilities.

For the happiness of all depends on the commitment of each to support both equality and individuality — both rights and responsibilities.

We declare all women to be mutually interdependent — banding together to support one another, sharing our experience, strength, and hope — that all may enjoy life, love, and the pursuit of laughter.

We agree to encourage one another in tough times and celebrate in good times.

We commit to taking turns leading and following,
inspiring and teaching, listening and learning.

We agree to give credit where credit is due —
including us.

We commit to loving ourselves first — because
we can't give what we don't have.

With this declaration of interdependence, we set
ourselves free... free from old beliefs that are
no longer true; free from self-doubt, insecurity,
and loneliness; free from self-imposed perfectionism.

We set ourselves free... heeding our intuition in all her
guises; loving our bodies through every change;
finding our voices to speak our own truths.

We set ourselves free... to create fulfilling work,
form nurturing families, and build great friendships.

We are strong; we are beautiful; we are generous;
we are wise.

We are women... committed to creating a world
that affirms us all.
                              — BJ Gallagher
                              and Lisa Hammond

🌀 Don't settle for "good enough"... keep learning, growing, and changing.

🌀 Follow your passion; appreciate your own self-worth.

🌀 You always have choices, and by not expressing your opinion, you are making a choice.

🌀 Be honest with yourself, as well as with others.

🌀 Give all you have without looking for something in return. Reach out for that which you can attain and not for that which is impossible. Be all you can, for only then will you awaken to the person you want to be. *(Joan Benicken)*

$\mathcal{M}$any people
go from one thing
to another
searching for happiness
but with each new venture
they find themselves
more confused
and less happy
until they discover
that what they are
searching for
is inside themselves
and what will make them happy
is sharing their real selves
with the one they love

— Susan Polis Schutz

*I*f you ever find yourself
chasing after the wrong
things, remember this — the love
between a family, and the
moments spent together with
your family and friends, are the
only answer to all that is crazy
in the world.

— Susan Polis Schutz

*A*ccomplishing your daily
goals has a place, but the
heart has a valid agenda of
its own. When you can look back
on a day and find within it even
one warm memory of a single
touching story, you've paid
attention to your heart. That's
worth whatever time it took.

— Victoria Moran

🌀 *Having someplace to go is home. Having someone to love is family. Having both is a blessing.* (Author Unknown)

🌀 *Cherish the times spent with family and loved ones. Those are the greatest memories you will ever make.*

🌀 *The greatest love of all is the love of a mother for her child.*

🌀 *The love of a family toward one another can mold one's attitude forever toward the world.* (Susan Polis Schutz)

🌀 *You will find as you look back upon your life that the moments that stand out, the moments when you have really lived, are the moments when you have done things in a spirit of love.* (Henry Drummond)

🌀 *Look for love all around you... in the eyes of a child, the touch of a pet, or the face of a stranger.*

🌀 *You can never say "I love you" too many times to the people you care about.*

🌀 *Sometimes a hug is the best medicine.*

🌀 *The love we give away is the only love we keep.* (Elbert Hubbard)

If you only knew how much love surrounds you every moment of every day! It comes from the most likely and unlikely places, in a never-ending stream of loving thoughts and loving gestures. You might not even be aware, though it's there all the same. Comforting you, washing over you, lifting you up even when you're looking in another direction. Even when you're feeling unloved and unlovable. Whether you know it or not, whether you believe it or not, you are loved. No question about it. You are loved.

— Rachel Snyder

🌀 You may not realize it, but you have
a lot of wisdom and experience to share.

🌀 Be a mentor to somebody.

🌀 There are people who look up to
you and depend on you.

🌀 What goes around comes around.

🌀 The praise and good feelings you give to
others will come back to you.

The priceless gifts we give each other
are not the ones wrapped
in fancy paper,
but the gifts we give when
we give of ourselves.
It is the love that we share.
It is the comfort we lend at times of need.
It is the moments we spend together
helping each other follow our dreams.
The most priceless gifts we can give
are the understanding and caring
that come from the heart.
And each and every one of us
has these gifts to offer...
through the gift of ourselves.

— Ben Daniels

The Six Most Important Things You Can Do

◎ Look in the mirror and smile... and see an amazing person looking back at you. You really are someone special, and your presence is a present to the world around you.

◎ When you're counting your blessings, be sure to include the privilege of having a new sunrise every morning and a brand-new beginning every day.

◎ Don't ever give up on your hopes and dreams. Your happiness is depending on you to stay strong.

🌀 *Know that you can reach deep inside and find everything you need to get through each moment that lies ahead.*

🌀 *When you talk to those who matter most, open the door to your heart. The wider it is, the easier it will be for things like compassion and understanding to come inside. And it just naturally follows... the more wonderful visitors you have, the more your life will shine.*

🌀 *Unwind a little and smile a lot and try not to worry too much. Know that you're loved and cared for... and that, whenever you need them, your guardian angels are great about working overtime.*

— Douglas Pagels

A beautiful person is someone who is caring and giving and gracious — someone whose smiles are like sunshine and laughter and whose words always seem to say the things you most like to hear — someone who lights up a room with radiance and who lights up every little corner of the world with a loveliness it has never known before.

— *Laine Parsons*

- *You are beautiful when you smile.*

- *You are beautiful when you laugh.*

- *You are beautiful when you stand up for what you believe.*

- *You are beautiful with or without makeup.*

- *You are beautiful when you are proud of your body — imperfections and all!*

- *You are beautiful when you speak and act from the heart.*

*W*e all become different people
as we grow older,
with different hopes and dreams,
goals and achievements,
memories and feelings.
No one can ever say that, as a person,
they are all they can be,
for it is then that they
have stopped growing from within.
We must continue to grow,
to dream,
to make new memories,
and to do whatever gives us peace
within ourselves.

— *Shirley Vander Pol*

🌀 *Feel good about your age, knowing it has nothing to do with who you are and everything to do with what you mean to others.* (Debbie Burton-Peddle)

🌀 *Every day is a gift; every moment is an opportunity to unwrap that gift.*

🌀 *Gray hair is earned — it's a reminder of all you've accomplished.*

🌀 *It is never too late to be what you might have been.* (George Eliot)

🌀 *Don't ever stop loving, don't ever stop believing, don't ever stop dreaming your dreams.* (Laine Parsons)

Every now and then,
we all need a little recognition
for the things we think no one notices...

You do wonderful things
on a daily basis to make others' lives easier.
Some may not think to say
those two simple words that, when expressed,
mean the world to another person.

So for the times when those two words go unspoken
or the times when things are moving too fast...
"Thank you."

Pat yourself on the back and smile,
because all your hard work and dedication
haven't gone unnoticed.

— Lamisha Serf

🌀 *You are the epitome of thoughtfulness and generosity.*

🌀 *No one could ever take your place.*

🌀 *You make a positive difference in the lives of countless people.*

🌀 *You deserve everything good that comes your way.*

🌀 *Thank you! Thank you! Thank you!*

🌀 *You're smart.*

🌀 *You're creative.*

🌀 *You're charismatic.*

🌀 *You're nurturing.*

🌀 *You're adventurous.*

🌀 *You're full of possibilities.*

🌀 *You're perfect just the way you are.*

You ou are a remarkable woman
who accomplishes so much
as a strong woman
in a man's world
You are strong but soft
strong but caring
strong but compassionate

You are a remarkable woman
who accomplishes so much
as a giving woman
in a selfish world
You give to your friends
to your family
to everyone

You are a remarkable woman
and you are loved by so many people
whose lives you have touched

— Susan Polis Schutz

🌀 *There is no one else on the planet like you, and there never will be.*

🌀 *You are a bright, talented, compassionate, one-of-a-kind, absolutely fantastic human being!*

🌀 *You bring cheer to so many people just by your presence in their lives.*

🌀 *The world is fortunate to have you in it.*

🌀 *You are loved and admired more than you'll ever know.*

*ou are amazing. You're treasured
and celebrated and quietly thanked. You
make so much sun shine through, and you
inspire so much joy in the lives of everyone
who is lucky enough to know you.*

*You are a very special person, giving so
many people a reason to smile. You deserve
to receive the best in return. May the
happiness you give away come back to
warm you each and every day of your life.*

— Sydney Nealson

Acknowledgments

We gratefully acknowledge the permission granted by the following authors, publishers, and authors' representatives to reprint poems or excerpts from their publications.

PrimaDonna Entertainment Corp. for "The greatest gift…" and "There will be times in life…" by Donna Fargo. Copyright © 2010, 2012 by PrimaDonna Entertainment Corp. All rights reserved.

April Aragam for "There is no one…." Copyright © 2012 by April Aragam. All rights reserved.

Random House, Inc., for "There is a vitality…" by Martha Graham from MARTHA: THE LIFE AND WORK OF MARTHA GRAHAM by Agnes De Mille. Copyright © 1956, 1991 by Agnes De Mille. All rights reserved.

Lisa Butler for "It's easy to get caught up…" and "There are times when…." Copyright © 2012 by Lisa Butler. All rights reserved.

Paula Finn for "Set a goal each day…." Copyright © 2012 by Paula Finn. All rights reserved.

Humanics Publishing Group for "Stretching herself too thin…" from THE TAO OF WOMEN, edited by Pamela K. Metz & Jacqueline L. Tobin. Copyright © 1995 by Brumby Holdings, Inc. All rights reserved.

Jacqueline Schiff for "Embrace change…." Copyright © 2012 by Jacqueline Schiff. All rights reserved.

Deanna Beisser for "There are two very easy things…" and "To be good at any one thing…." Copyright © 2012 by Deanna Beisser. All rights reserved.

Doubleday, a division of Random House, Inc., for "There's only one rule…" from THE DIARY OF A YOUNG GIRL: THE DEFINITIVE EDITION by Anne Frank. Otto H. Frank & Mirjam Presser, Editors, translated by Susan Massotty. English translation copyright © 1995, 2001 by Doubleday, a division of Random House, Inc. All rights reserved.

Jeanie Turocy for "By turning your disappointments…." Copyright © 2012 by Jeanie Turocy. All rights reserved.

Robin Magon for "Gather up your doubts…." Copyright © 2012 by Robin Magon. All rights reserved.

Candy Paull for "There are angels among us." Copyright © 2012 by Candy Paull. All rights reserved.

Linda E. Knight for "Try to do these things every day…." Copyright © 2012 by Linda E. Knight. All rights reserved.

Jason Blume for "The things that matter…." Copyright © 2012 by Jason Blume. All rights reserved.

Melody Beattie and the Hazelden Foundation for "Gratitude unlocks the fullness of life" from GRATITUDE: AFFIRMING THE GOOD THINGS IN LIFE by Melody Beattie. Copyright © 1992 by Melody Beattie. All rights reserved.

Barbara J. Hall for "So often, it's the little things…." Copyright © 2012 by Barbara J. Hall. All rights reserved.

Conari Press, an imprint of Red Wheel/Weiser, LLC, www.redwheelweiser.com, for "It's so easy for women…" from WOMEN'S WORK IS NEVER DONE by BJ Gallagher. Copyright © 2006 by BJ Gallagher. All rights reserved.

BJ Gallagher for "Women's Declaration of Interdependence" by BJ Gallagher and Lisa Hammond (HuffingtonPost.com: June 29, 2010). Copyright © 2010 by BJ Gallagher. All rights reserved.

HarperCollins Publishers for "When you can look back…" from CREATING A CHARMED LIFE: SENSIBLE, SPIRITUAL SECRETS EVERY BUSY WOMAN SHOULD KNOW by Victoria Moran. Copyright © 1999 by Victoria Moran. All rights reserved.

Rachel Snyder for "If you only knew…." Copyright © 2012 by Rachel Snyder. All rights reserved.

A careful effort has been made to trace the ownership of selections used in this anthology in order to obtain permission to reprint copyrighted material and give proper credit to the copyright owners. If any error or omission has occurred, it is completely inadvertent, and we would like to make corrections in future editions provided that written notification is made to the publisher:

BLUE MOUNTAIN ARTS, INC., P.O. Box 4549, Boulder, Colorado 80306.